you are enough

you are enough

a small anthology

small robin press

you are enough: a small anthology

Editors: Erin Michaela Sweeney, Cheshir, and Robin Taylor
Cover design: Robin Cangie and Robin Taylor
Book design: Robin Taylor
Cover artwork: Kate Brennan
(*materials include crayons, hair dryer, sheer determination*)

Printed in the United States of America
ISBN 979-8-9996260-0-4

small robin press
Edmonds, WA

SmallRobinPress.com

Contents

Foreword

Growth. We're pushed to grow from the moment we emerge into the world. Bigger is better. Size matters. Go big or go home.

As writers, as authors, we are told that growing an audience is essential to making our mark. We need visibility, growth metrics, positive stats, all for the sake of demonstrating... what, exactly? Is it really better to be big? Are our words more meaningful if our audience is large? Is this how we measure success?

In defiance of growth, would anyone choose to stay small? What would that look like? How could a small mindset impact our writing?

In early 2024 I asked how others felt about having a "small" focus. That simple question launched the creation of a community space—SmallStack—built around choosing and staying small and embodying an intentionally small approach. SmallStack then opened a submission process soliciting guest posts from our online audience. Writers were asked to speak their own small truths to help us find the edges and contours of this new, small community, and the creative explorations from them flooded in. We read stories about friendships between writer and commenter, journeys made possible for readers with compromised immune systems, and the discovery of our own significance by de-centering the voices around us.

It was no simple task to sort through so many brilliant, compelling ideas. This is, after all, the entire point of being—*and staying*—small; that we cannot bring every loved object on our journey, and so we must choose wisely as we consider the path ahead. Selecting essays was the beginning of longer relationships with our authors. If you've been through the editing process, you know how much you learn about yourself along the way, and we benefitted from that exploration, too. We fell in love with our authors' words, helped them refine their voices, and watched from the sidelines as our small crowd of supporters cheered them on.

The essays published here were originally chosen as part of a guest post series on SmallStack, an emerging online community. In their original form, each essay was a web post and a newsletter to our community. Supporters and friends filled the comments with messages of understanding and kinship.

"All we have is small," by Jamie Wallace, chips away at the barriers we construct around perfection and how long it takes to achieve our own impressions of success. Alexa Spiegel's "Is Substack better than therapy," and Amanda Gibson's "A new diagnosis" each tackle how we heal through our connections with others, even—especially—when that healing challenges our identity.

"Small is where the best connections are made," by Sarah Teresa Cook, "Enough to be happy," by Kate Brennan, and "Beyond questions big and small" by Sarah Sadie use introspection and delightful imagery in embracing small as its own choice in the face of growth metrics. They help us view the world through the lens of laughter, wonder, and gratitude.

Would any book about small stories be complete without a bakery and a moment spent in wonder at how monkeys and humans form friendship through communication? Rachel Shenk's "The stay small recipe," and Dr. Sanjida O'Connell's "What monkeys can tell us about community" show us that hunger and curiosity brighten our journey of discovery toward understanding small.

These original essays defined us, shaped us, and told the world who we were growing to become. As each story was shared, more members of the community found us and found themselves. We formed friendships, shared grief, learned to embody joy, and embraced the challenges of "being small" together. Newer writers came forward with hope that their contributions mattered in a place that valued small. Established authors provided mentoring, encouragement, and praise.

Once that project was complete, the community asked over and over, "When will you re-open the submissions for guest posts?" We had found a need to fill. The next logical step was to do something bigger—but not too big—to demonstrate the power of small writers banding together with shared purpose.

Publishing our writing is a dream we share across our vast intersectional community. Some of us hope for a book deal for a memoir, others bravely take publishing into our own hands. We pitch to magazines and journals, we enter contests. We write, and we write. We edit out thousands of words, then we hold our breath as friends read our souls written on paper. We entrust our fate to emails and form entries, and we try not to take rejection too personally. We dream about book covers, graphic design, and dust jacket blurbs, and we wonder what reviewers will be quoted saying on the backs of our books.

But the barriers for many of us are enormous. They are exhausting to confront. We feel excluded and erased. Our voices are just too small to be found. The Publishing Industrial Complex isn't a kind or welcoming place for small writers or those of us from marginalized communities, especially those of us who are disabled, neurodiverse, queer, immigrants, or intersectional and complex.

Small Robin Press was born in response to this frustration and the shared struggle so many of us face in getting our work published. See a pathway, make a difference, right? And as easy as that, our publishing future began.

Small Robin Press was built one thread at a time. Some of those threads came from our own experiences with the publishing world, others came from stories that were shared or passed down. We see you, Publishing Industrial Complex, but we know you don't see us. And we know, deep down, that the way this industry is built is toxic, extractive, and flawed. So we've created something different, something softer and kinder, something open and willing to say yes to small voices with big stories to tell.

The story of our press is not unlike the stories of other small treasures in the pages of this book. Our beginnings are small, our dreams are expansive, and our gratitude is vast.

Our call to the community to create something new, sincere, and insightful about being small brought many carefully crafted essays into our hands. This book is a celebration of that work. More than that, it is our own small beginning in the world of publishing as an independent press. We would not be here without our authors, and so we owe them more than this book can possibly express.

Eight of our guest post authors join us here, each having crafted uniquely touching pieces about love, acceptance, grief, joy, creativity, and community. These words, given so graciously, helped fashion the very shape of who we are today and who we will grow to be tomorrow. I am immensely grateful to each of our authors for the time and love they poured into this process alongside us.

What a beautiful beginning to our story.

Robin Taylor, Small Robin Press Co-Founder

All we have is small

by Jamie Wallace

When you first arrive on Substack, it can feel a little like walking into a very large party that's been in full swing for some time. There are a LOT of people here, including more than a few household names—I'm looking at you George Saunders, Elizabeth Gilbert, Heather Cox Richardson, and Dan Rather—a treasure trove of highly successful writers (each with their own devoted fanbase), and an ever-growing cadre of Substack superstars who gain subscribers like the pinball wizard racking up points.

It can be overwhelming. It can be intimidating. It can even be a little discouraging. Especially if you're a "nobody" who is starting from scratch. Even for folks who are just here to engage as readers, it's a lot. Some days, it feels like standing at the bottom of Mount Everest without a sherpa in sight. And you're dressed for a cocktail party, not a mountaineering expedition.

It's okay. Don't worry. A big part of what makes Substack so appealing to both writers and readers is that it is built for direct connection. The algorithm wasn't created to promote pay-to-play or system-gaming strategies. It's intentionally designed (and I hope this never changes) to encourage and support actual human connection and collaboration.

It reminds me of blogging back in the old days, circa 2007. In a weird way, my divorce was the catalyst behind my blogging career. I had no preexisting network; I just started posting about my experience on an indie parenting site called *Maya's Mom*. I connected 1:1 with readers in the comments. The editors noticed and invited me to join their staff. Soon after, Maya's Mom was bought by Baby-Center (an enormous parenting brand), and the rest is, as they say, history.

While still writing for BabyCenter, I joined two other collaborative blogs—one about business-to-business marketing called *Savvy B2B* (we called ourselves the "Savvy Sisters"), and another about writing called the *New Hampshire Writers Network* (NHWN). This was before Twitter was a hot mess or Facebook had become Meta and was trying to run our lives with a megalomaniac algorithm. The internet was a kinder, gentler place back then. It was less competition and more collaboration.

I noticed a similar vibe at Substack right from the start, and I'm not the only one. Writers like me who were blogging back in the day get a little misty eyed when they first arrive on Substack because it feels a bit like a home we thought we'd never see again.

But let's be clear. Yes, Substack the platform offers writers and readers much better tools than we could ever have dreamed. (No offense, WordPress.) But it's the humans who hang out here who bring that old-school feeling to the place.

Here are just a few of the things I've heard repeatedly from fellow OG bloggers who have discovered Substack Land.

Everyone here is so welcoming

Even though I am a tiny fish in this huge (and growing!) pond, I have found everyone here to be very approachable. Just like in the early days of blogging, even folks who've already built big audiences are really engaged with their readers. I was absolutely tickled the first time Tom Cox restacked one of my comments. It felt really good to be noticed and included.

So many people are open to collaboration

The three blogs I wrote for back in the day were all collaborative projects. We cowrote posts, guest posted all over the place, and accepted guest posts on our sites. We cross-promoted each other's work as well as the work of our so-called competitors. I've found a similar ethos here on Substack. Shortly after launching *Inner Wilderness Unlimited*, I connected in the comments with another writer who invited me to be part of an interview series on her Substack.

People are so genuine in their support

People seemed more engaged in the early days of blogging—maybe because the scene was new and our content feeds felt more like a babbling brook than a firehose. Since then, most social media interactions have become a bit less... authentic. Here on Substack, however, readers leave super thoughtful comments, restack with context, and even send private messages of support. I have used Substack's DM feature to connect with other writers who have been really grateful for a behind-the-scenes boost of encouragement.

Everyone is so inspiring

There are so many great writers on Substack. You can let that intimidate you or inspire you. As bloggers, we used to quote each other and link to each other's blogs all the time. I see similar linking and attribution happening on Substack and employed it myself in my post "Give me all them guilty pleasures." It's a beautifully organic conversation that spans the whole network rather than being isolated on one Substack.

These are my people

One of the best things about the Substack community is the opportunity to make real friends. When a post I never intended to write—"All humans are lonely"—got more traction than I'd expected, I realized that a lot of us are on Substack to make authentic connections. The Substack community gave me the courage to share some truly personal experiences, and I'm so glad I did. Years after our blogging partnerships ended, I am still friends with several of my fellow writers from *Savvy B2B* and *NHWN*. Forged in the fires of a shared journey, our relationships have endured. I am delighted to be sharing this journey with writers here on Substack, and definitely feel like new friendships are blossoming. This matters to me because, as Drew Holcomb sings, "You gotta find your people, then you'll find yourself." Yes, you do; and yes, you will.

So, let's head back into that big party that felt so overwhelming and intimidating.

Here's the thing: You don't walk into a party, grab a mic, and start addressing the entire room. That would be weird. Instead, you mingle and have conversations with a few people at a time.

The goal isn't to put yourself center stage and try to grab everyone's attention. Your goal is to host a party within the party. You want to create a little group of folks who are hanging out in the kitchen, on the porch, by the fireplace, or around the piano. Your group is not separate from the larger party. In fact, it's natural for people to move between groups and cross-pollinate the conversation by making new introductions.

The magic is not in some grand plan, splashy entrance, or big-deal moment. It's in the small gestures and kindnesses between you and another person. It's in choosing one simple, small thing to do: extend a hand, show a little love, share something, add to the conversation. You know; like, comment, restack.

On their own, each of these actions is tiny, the product of a few moments. But cumulatively, they help create a space that is genuinely welcoming, encouraging, collaborative, and inspiring—one that helps each of us become a better writer, reader, and community member.

The beautiful thing about focusing on one small action at a time? It's a strategy you can apply to pretty much everything in your life. When you think about it, it's obvious that every Big Thing starts out as a small thing: a whisper of an idea, a quiet "what if." The mightiest oak starts as a tiny acorn.

And the only way to make progress on our Big Dreams is to take one small step at a time. Every book is written one word at a time. Every relationship is built one moment at a time. Every marathon is run one stride at a time.

A thriving Substack is built on a foundation of taking small, consistent steps in your own work and making small, authentic connections with others who are journeying alongside you.

You don't need to overthink it. Just do what feels kind and generous. You may be surprised at how far that will take you.

Is Substack better than therapy?

by Alexa Spiegel

I have never been one to share my life on the internet. I consider myself a deeply private person. My social media is 90% pictures of my cat. How is it, then, that last year I found myself publishing explicit details about my mental health on Substack, details I had yet to divulge to my closest family or (in some cases) my therapist?

Let me back up. I was 12 years into a successful corporate career and deeply unhappy. For years I'd set aside my own values in pursuit of praise and productivity. But acting in discordance with your values has consequences.

By early 2023, I'd developed a persistent tightness in my chest. I learned a new word: anxiety. And yet I pressed on, showing up to every meeting with a detailed agenda and a smile on my face.

This feeling built and built, a pressure cooker of repressed emotion until, eventually, I fell apart. Once the tears started, they wouldn't stop. I spent a week in bed. I took time off work. I was privileged to have the support of my partner and family, who helped me get back into therapy. I learned another new word: depression.

Ultimately, I quit my high-paying, 401(k)-matching "everything I'd been told to want" job with zero plan for what came next.

Shaky and unsteady, my sense of self lying in fragmented pieces on the floor, I reached for one of the oldest tools in my toolbox: writing. Everything that had been trapped beneath the surface rushed up: a tsunami of doubt, insecurity, anger, and sadness. Writing it down felt like an exorcism in the best way, and the tightness in my chest slowly began to ease.

Still, I felt a deep-seated urge to do something more. I spoke to a writer friend to learn more about Substack. When she told me how she was writing a newsletter about her struggles with fertility, baring intimate details to strangers in beautiful, long-form essays, I thought, now that's brave. If she can do it, maybe I can, too.

I leapt, unsure of where or how I would land.

Less than two weeks after quitting my job, I created a Substack account, taught myself how to use Canva, designed my newsletter, and drafted my first post.

When I published my first newsletter, I felt like I was going to throw up.

Clinging to a single shred of bravery, I did it almost without thinking, afraid that if I thought about it too much (What will they think! What will they say!) I would chicken out. Instead, I was desperate to know what it would feel like to finally reveal my innermost thoughts and feelings. To hold them up to the light as if to say, "See! Here's all the ways I'm broken!"

Then the messages started to pour in.

I'm so proud of you.

I had no idea you were going through this.

I had a similar experience last year.

Thank you so much for sharing.

Relief flooded my nervous system, accompanied by a warm fuzzy feeling. Two mental messages arrived, breaking through the surface of my consciousness with speed and clarity: I'm not alone, and I still have value. The initial support was overwhelming and bolstered my confidence.

That first newsletter invariably altered me. It was as if I had cracked open a Pandora's box of emotion, and I wanted to get it all out of my body. I couldn't write my next newsletter fast enough.

The millennial muse Lena Dunham once shared this sage advice: "Find the story only you can tell, and make it on the scale you can make it." I've taken that direction perhaps too literally, but unfortunately (or fortunately), I don't know much about fall-inspired recipes, where to find the perfect vintage candlesticks, or the best TV to watch this month. What I do know is my own journey with mental health. I know about burnout, anxiety, depression, and all the ways in which we can fall apart.

In my Substack I explore grief, boundaries, coping skills, generational trauma, and self-compassion. True to form I never overthink it; whatever comes out, I hold myself accountable to publishing it (grammatical errors and all). What at first felt scary now feels invigorating: a vulnerability cold plunge that shocks my entire system and floods me with icy dopamine. Zing!

One thing I've learned is that vulnerability is addictive. More than the likes, the comments, the follows (although, let's be honest, those are all very nice), it's the sharing that acts as my primary reward system.

Writing on its own is therapeutic, yes, but sharing my writing has brought the greatest gifts. The sense of community, of belonging, of universal humanness is enough to bring me to my knees in gratitude.

Every "I feel like that too..." or "This really resonated with me..." serves to validate why I include such personal details. If writing is the tool, connection is the goal.

Thanks to Substack, I've reconnected with relatives from other states and childhood friends. They've sent messages about how my writing has affected them. In one case a friend texted, "You've inspired me to start writing again." She's since launched her own Substack, a heartwarming affirmation of how one brave act leads to another.

Similarly, Substack has opened the door to more honest, vulnerable conversations with the people I'm closest to, resulting in deeper, more profound connections. I find myself craving more of this intimacy; less "tell me about your weekend" and more "tell me about your mental health."

There is something magical about the Substack community in contrast to other forms of social media. It's safe and cozy, like wrapping up in a warm blanket of human connection. Through Substack I've built a support network—especially my new writing group—that I can turn to for empathy and understanding.

There are downsides to being so vulnerable, of course. When I publish some of my most personal material, I often forget I'm writing for an internet of strangers and not just my mom. The first time someone I didn't personally know subscribed to *Sundays in high school,* I felt a jolt of fear. The seal had been broken.

I struggle with the balance of writing about the people in my life and, at the same time, wanting to protect their privacy. I have moments of discomfort, realizing that an old work colleague might take offense to my version of events. Looking back, I often cringe at some of the details in early newsletters.

Substack is also a digital diary of my healing. It captures my peaks and valleys: struggling with self-doubt one week, learning to be kinder to myself another. Each newsletter serves as a sort of emotional time capsule. When strung together, the chronological change over time be-comes clear. In moments of crisis, I can look back, reflect, and see how far I've come. And it's a long way, indeed.

I credit my Substack with my recovery and self-discovery as much as I do my regular therapy sessions. (Plus, as a bonus, it's free.) It has given me confidence, a soft place to land, an opportunity to tap back into my own creativity, and an excuse to talk ad nauseam about my experience, which in turn has allowed me to process it more fully.

If I were to lose all my (162!) subscribers tomorrow, I would still be here, writing and publishing. Not for them, not for the engagement, but for me. A purely, deliciously selfish act. One of the single most important things I do for my mental health.

I never thought of myself as someone who would en-dorse "healing out loud," but here I am, divulging my most vulnerable thoughts to an internet full of strangers on a weekly basis. And it's changed my life for the better.

So, what are you waiting for? Take the plunge right now. Be messy and brave and honest. Trust that the Small-Stack community is here for you with kindness, respect, and support.

And believe me when I say the benefits of being vulner-able are nothing short of magic.

Enough to be happy

by Kate Brennan

A decade ago, I attended an art show on Happiness. It was a statistical wonderland of installation and interactive art nestled somewhere in the heart of West Philly. I vaguely recall something involving popsicle sticks; I vaguely recall a spinning wheel. There was a bike you could pedal to light up a sign. It felt slightly transgressive and slightly novel. With a certain amount of physical effort, something like "Be the change" or "Reduce, Reuse, Recycle" or "Coors Light" lit up in neon letters across the wall. There were little uppers and downers listed by the elevator buttons.

I remember so little, from the exhibit and from life in general. But I do remember this: One of the pieces examined Happiness based on income and concluded that money actually could buy happiness. Up to $74,000.

More than that, and money was no longer related to happiness at all. But it wasn't really the money that secured happiness. It was the money that secured housing, sustenance, education, health care, stability. It was the money that allowed people to live and work in a way that allowed them to continue to live and work the next year and the year after that. They determined that $74k could provide a sustainable life.

The number has undoubtedly changed since ten years ago. (And let's be honest, it's possibly an annual income many of us have never seen.) The number probably fluctuates based on household size, cost of living, and phases of the moon. But what matters is not the number itself; what matters is that there is a number at all. There is a proven threshold. There is a tipping point at which a certain amount of money is enough for what we all claim to be after.

Because don't we all just want to be happy?

When Robin posed the SmallStack question, Do you want to stay small or grow? My initial thought was, Grow! Of course, grow! But when I started reflecting on the why, I couldn't actually find the thread. I suppose I want to grow... to enough. But what does that mean? What is enough? Five hundred subscribers? One thousand? Ten thousand?

There is a proven threshold. There is a tipping point at which a certain amount of money is enough for what we all claim to be after.

Lately, I feel like I'm drowning in a world of too much. There must be enough—I am in the constant state of slogging through it all! Emails, notifications, real mail, meetings, portals, texts, messages, stuff—this grating minutiae of life. Most days, I feel like I'm flailing in a ball pit or flying in a bad dream: paddle as I might, my little duck legs will not move me forward.

Once I saw a show about a couple in Japan who had renovated the back of their truck and lived inside it. She gestured to the mat they rolled out to sleep on; he demonstrated how they cook with the hot pot. Life was getting too complicated; it shouldn't be that complicated, she said.

But where do you bathe? The interviewer asked.

There are lakes; there are streams.

I think about that couple as my webbed feet thrash. She's right. Life's too complicated. It has become so complicated, in fact, I am not sure our fragile human souls were meant to assail the constant bedlam. It is so muddled, I find it difficult to see the forest for the trees amidst the deluge of information, of email, of BOGOs, of advertisements. It is so knotted, I sometimes cannot disentangle what I feel is true from the tentacles of a world that prioritizes plastic over people and guns over children. Many of the values of the world are not my values, and yet, I have to live in the world regardless. I have to survive here. So do you.

So how do we protect and preserve our best, most sacred creative selves whilst trying to climb out of the germy plastic ball pit that is the world? And more than that, how do we not just survive a world with values we don't espouse, but create a world with ones we do?

Why was my knee-jerk reaction grow, grow, grow? I don't even like large parties!

What if there is a tipping point to enough?

My initial response was born of the constant barrage of bigger, better, best—of more, faster, harder. It was tied to busy-ness and business, to technology, to #success, #lifegoals, #grateful. It was megabytes and megastores selling a life, along with the idea that it was a life I wanted.

Because if happiness is truly the goal, and there is more than enough, then why the heck aren't we all elated?

Maybe we don't actually want what the world is offering with its exhausting pace and rampant burnout. Maybe we want a life that is wholly our own, cultivated with thoughtfulness, curiosity, and sustainability for the people we hope to become. Maybe we deserve it too.

In Don Miguel Ruiz's book on Toltec Wisdom, *The Four Agreements*, the Fourth Agreement is "Do Your Best." I always associate this concept with enough. It lives in the solar plexus, tumbling around with identity, productivity, responsibility, energy, effort, and ego.

"If you try too hard to do more than your best, you will spend more energy than is needed and in the end your best will not be enough. When you overdo, you deplete your body and go against yourself."

What if there is a tipping point to enough? What if accumulation at some point leads to depletion? It makes me think of living in a larger house than is necessary. At what point does your home shift from being a haven of comfort to a stressor filled with junk that doesn't bring you joy? At what point does your home—or anything—start sapping the energy it was meant to restore?

And it makes me wonder: Do we want 1,000 subscribers who don't read our work or 100 who do? Do we want 2,500 free readers or 25 who think our work is worth paying for? Do we want 500 in a community who will never engage or 50 who are consistent, thoughtful, and invested? The metrics of the internet have us so seduced by quantity, but didn't we start the work for its quality?

It is hard to confront the topic of enough. What if less is actually enough? What if all the pushing—the Type A-achievement-driven persona, the effort, the excelling, the grades, the drive, the energy, the force, the ferocity, the fighting—what if it isn't getting me closer to who I want to be, but driving me away?

What if the only thing standing between me and enough to be happy is, in fact... me?

Ruiz states, "Doing your best is taking the action because you love it, not because you're expecting a reward." For those of us who grapple with the concept of doing enough, having enough, creating enough, writing enough, marketing enough, networking enough, investing enough, saving enough, giving enough, trying enough, being enough—this is the quintessential truth. This is the joy, the pleasure, the essence, the eternal thread: Doing the thing for the sake of doing the thing. For the love of the work. For the person you become while doing it.

What is enough to be happy?

I am.

I am enough.

And so are you.

A new diagnosis

by Amanda Gibson

Someone asked me a great question the other day, 'What chapter of your life are you in at the moment?' A year ago I would have snapped back, 'My rock-bottom chapter,' but now I would honestly (and more politely) reply, 'My healing chapter.'

On the 30th January 2024, I was officially diagnosed with the chronic autoimmune disease ankylosing spondylitis (AS). It is a type of inflammatory arthritis that mainly affects the spine and pelvis but can also affect many other parts of the body like the heart, lungs, skin, and bowels.

For me, it comes in debilitating waves. My body flares up with an intense pain that I can only describe as broken glass stabbing at my joints. The soul-crushing fatigue is never far behind, which leaves me drained of any energy or hope. The only thing I can do is to lie in bed and surrender myself to it. I shut out the light, the noise, and any move-ment. Days, sometimes weeks, pass as I desperately wait for a sense of normality to return. The not-knowing is the worst part. A doubt creeps in. I get scared that I may lose myself in this void forever, but I always come back, even-tually.

It took me nearly ten years to get this diagnosis. I spent many years searching and fighting for an answer to my pain, frantically trying to figure out why I was drowning in these waves. I knew something was desperately wrong in my body, but no one could tell me why. I turned to the healthcare system, the very system that was supposed to help, but was often dismissed. They told me I was 'just anxious.' yet never offered any substantial solutions.

After telling me over the telephone I had ankylosing spondylitis, a life-altering disease, my rheumatologist di-rected me to a website. 'It will tell you everything you need to know.'

'Thanks?' I said before hanging up.

My head still pounded with a weird mix of relief, confu-sion, and grief as I skimmed the site. One statistic in par-ticular popped out at me:

It takes on average 8.5 years for ankylosing spondylitis to be diagnosed in the UK.

Why does it take this long? It felt like a slap in the face. I stopped reading before the hatred burnt through my body like a wildfire. I could feel myself start to drain of en-ergy and go limp under the weight of our collective sadness. You see, I'm not a statistical anomaly. My story is one of many.

One in ten individuals will get diagnosed with some form of autoimmune disease in their lifetime. 80% of these are women. However, I have read countless stories of others being ignored, tales of medical gaslighting, of delays in diagnosis, of near-death experiences, all because no one truly listens to our stories.

I have now started to heal my body, but the pain of being ignored for so long has left its mark. To unravel that much hurt may take a lifetime to fix.

They say healing isn't linear, but what do they mean by healing in the first place? Healing is defined as 'to make free from injury or disease'; 'to make well again'; 'to restore to health.'

But what if you have a chronic illness? There is no cure. There is no going back to 100% health.

Over time I have come to find that healing can be seen as an ongoing process, one that may span many chapters of a lifetime.

In this past year, I have found healing in a variety of places. I expected to find healing in therapy, exercise, and healthy eating. But one place surprised me... here on Substack.

I would like to take this opportunity to share my gratitude with the community that is helping me, and others like me, to heal.

You make me feel less alone.

As someone with a chronic illness, I spend an inordinate amount of time in my bed resting, separated from the outside world. It would be very easy to just disappear. Pain and fatigue make me feel like a ghost of my former self. It's hard to reach out and join society.

When you withdraw, others withdraw from you.

Substack has given me the gift of connection again.

We help each other feel seen.

Not merely in likes or an accumulation of subscribers (although it's always nice), but more in the way that I see parts of myself echoed in others. Someone feels like I do! I'm not alone. Hurray!

Powerful healing happens within a community.

You expand my knowledge and understanding.

I love the myriad ways we can contribute to this collective healing.

Francesca Bossert (author of *Just For Fun*) with her humorous poems and positivity, Amber Horrox (author of *Warrior Within*) with her wealth of wisdom from her long journey to holistic health, Broadwaybabyto (author of *The Disabled Ginger*) teaching us how to be strong advocates, and Victoria Chin, MBA (author of *Carer Mentor: Empathy & Inspiration*), reminding us of the love and hard work of the carers of the ill. And so many more...

Empathy grows when we listen to one another.

You give me purpose again.

Being so ill eventually meant that I had to give up on my dream of being a nurse. When I was first diagnosed, I was stricken with grief for a life I wasn't going to have anymore. But seeing others with illness have such beautiful, meaningful lives, who are helping those around them by sharing their stories, has given me hope.

Could I help make people feel less alone in their own struggles?

Stories can inspire and give us hope.

You show me the strength in vulnerability.

I see the dedication from my readers, how they show up each and every week to read my posts. It's taught me to trust again.

Each week I tremble as I press post. Was I being too vulnerable this time? Will anyone read it? But each and every time I trust fall, they catch me.

People can hold feelings here, even the big scary emotions like sadness, grief, and anger. As a highly sensitive person, I've always been told I'm 'too sensitive,' 'too emotional,' 'too deep.' But here people crave authenticity and vulnerability because they know that is the way to true connection.

People I've never met in person have told me they are proud of me for writing how I really feel and how deeply they relate to what I have said. They thank me for sharing. Their words have meant so much to me, and I will always treasure their kindness.

We build trust and connection by reading each other's stories.

You remind me of my voice.

It took me many years of fighting to be heard to get my diagnosis. I often wanted to give up, too tired of fighting. Other people's stories gave me the courage, the strength, the knowledge to speak up.

When I first read Ruth Elliot-Booth's story (author of *Becoming Me*, a fellow AS Substacker), and how she was 'learning to take up space' again after her diagnosis, it encouraged me to do the same. The shame of being 'different' that I had held on to for so long slowly dissolved away with each passing paragraph of our shared story.

Telling my own story has helped me to accept myself as I am, chronic illness and all. I trust my own voice again.

I've started to see this diagnosis, instead of an ending, as just a new chapter in my life's story.

The stories we tell ourselves matter.

You are creating a community for people with chronic illnesses.

All the Substacks on chronic illness have taught me that we are worthy of love, of care, of a place in this world, to have a voice, even when it's cracked with pain and quiet with fatigue.

I appreciate that we are a small community. I feel like we're a bunch of lovable misfits, like 'The Goonies' gang or 'The Breakfast Club.' We've all just been longing to find our tribe of open souls, letting out our vulnerability in a safe space.

We are creating a beautiful little community here.

We are all healing each other, one word, one chapter, one story at a time.

So thank you to each and every person that has been brave enough to share their story of chronic illness and to those that care enough to read our stories.

Beyond questions big and small

by Sarah Sadie

Hello beautiful human. That's how I start each of my daily letters to the world, my "small made things," and by now it's habit and comfort, both. As I begin this essay, partly to get past the block of a blank screen and into the roll and flow of language, I imagine us, you and me, sitting across a table from each other in some café or coffee shop, sharing our stories and notes. Because we're all seekers, readers, hunters and gatherers, sharing experiences and signs along the way. What works? What helps? What should we look out for?

Although it's strange to me to admit this, since in my heart I'm still a beginner with each new page, I've been writing a loooong time. Decades. It's true I'm new here (I created *An Inviting Space* February 1 of 2024). I knew about Substack for a while, even subscribed to a few publications, but I didn't think about creating my own until recently. I started very small, promising myself I'd try it for a month (which happened to be the shortest month of the year). Now it's the start of a new school year, and here I still am, astonished to be here. Delighted. Intrigued. Grateful.

But let me back up and introduce myself. (This is one of the things I love about this platform, the space and invitation to digress, back up, reverse, noodle around, riff and experiment with theme and variation. We live in what feels like a rather flat and declarative time, but around here we can play and expand what's possible. Opening ourselves back up into language and complexity. I've learned by now the path through life for any of us is not linear. Maybe the writing and expression shouldn't be either?)

Hello. My name is Sarah.

I'm a poet and writer who stopped writing altogether for a few years in order to explore other roles: community builder, creativity coach, dance teacher, workshop and circle facilitator, entrepreneur. I wrote a lot in those roles but didn't count much of it as "writing," as I wasn't wearing the same hat and didn't feel the same freedom to lose myself into language.

There are many ways to talk about why I stopped writing. Maybe the easiest choice for this morning: I had said all I had to say in that phase of life. I'd exhausted my subject matter thoroughly and needed to wait until I was in a new place with new windows and views. Well, between life and me, we made that happen. Now, in a new house, new community, with graduated kids and a divorce under the bridge, I have time and reason to ask once again:

Where am I? How did I get here? What's the news from the backyard this morning?

Those feel like simple questions. But transitions and transformations can be difficult passages with plenty of grief and confusion. My journal felt heavy. Sometime in mid-January of this year, I began to wonder what it would feel like to recover delight and enjoyment. To find fun again. Here's a few lines captured from the pages of my January 15—16 entry:

"I'm at Pause as I consider how to become creative again with welcome, shelter, invitation and wild wonder. Today what comes up is a Substack around waging peace and hope. Each day a brief prompt or invitation. Listen to someone's story. Say thank you to your feet. Etc."

I kept writing into the possibility:

How does that feel in my body? I notice an uplift in my core. Solar plexus. A slight buzz in my head. Possibilities, ease. My feet start to stretch. My body likes this idea. There's room for humor, hope, fierce resilience. There's room for balm and calm... How to start small? How to start so small it feels sustainable?

I noticed how I started with a desire for smallness, and also, a wish to connect with others through prompts and encouragement. It wasn't so much about the writing as it was about reaching out to find other like-minded, like-hearted people. Looking back, I can see how I'd lost connection to my interior places, partly because of dramatic life events, partly because I'd been exploring many other roles that took me away from the private deep forests of mind that every writer must tend and attend. Last winter, I started with my feet and, day by day, returned to my body, my situation, understanding where I was in the world quite literally.

I began to work out where my boundaries existed. What did I want to say? How did I want to say it? What did I want to hold private?

One word at a time, I slowly began to put myself back together again. I explored Substack, read the work of others, and eagerly subscribed. I noticed that I was enjoying reading again. I kept writing, sending my "small made things" out into the world. My focus shifted from expanding beyond simple prompts and suggestions for my readership and myself, to noticing the world and reporting back on both exterior and interior wanderings. At the same time my sentences grew longer, more complex. My themes expanded and morphed. I discovered ways to write about all the things I had not been able to say for so long.

An Inviting Space invited me back to language, to remember passion and curiosity, and to rediscover myself as a writer. Over the days and months, without realizing it, or knowing what I was doing at the time, I fell in love with the world of writing all over again.

As of yet, there is no ending to this story. I'm still in the middle of the muddle. I'm still emerging. I'm still growing. I'm still figuring all of this out.

Maybe you are too?

What I notice now as a dedicated and (still) very small stacker: there's an inherent tension I feel pulling at me. And I suspect this is a tension that all creatives can relate to, no matter our chosen medium or craft.

On the one hand, I want to stay small as I started out. It's the place "where everybody knows your name," as the old Cheers song put it. There's a sense of shelter, protection, and safety in being small. It's a private playground with very low stakes. I can mess up. I can send out my rough drafts and not worry too much. It's also a completely supportive and friendly space. These readers are here, reading my words because they know me already. They care about me. I'm writing to friends. Which means I feel safe to be more intimate in what I share, if I choose. I can be vulnerable with less risk.

For me, staying small means staying real. Keeping myself honest, reminding myself to remain vulnerable.

Yet, on the other hand... I want to grow. I, too, feel the pull and attraction of all those "How I Increased My Readership" and "How I Went from 20 to 2,000 Subscribers in a Month" articles. I click into most of them. I've considered signing up for programs and mentors who specifically target audience growth. Maybe I still will.

Why would I do this?

Here across the imaginary table from you, let me explore my answers, be honest and vulnerable for a moment.

There are practical reasons to want to grow bigger, such as wanting more money for my writing (no shame in that). The math is pretty simple: to get more paid subscribers I need more subscribers, period. Also, paid or not, I do want more readers. Doesn't every writer on some level want more people reading her work? Maybe it's the Leo in me, but I want to be part of the party and part of the conversation. I want more scope and influence in my chosen platform. I want my voice to matter in some way. And in order to matter, it has to be heard.

Dear Reader, I want to be heard. Don't you?

Playwrights want to fill the theater. Musicians want to maximize their downloads. Chefs want waiting lists for tables. We all want buzz. Surely this isn't unusual or unexpected, even if it is uncomfortable at times.

If you're like me, those two opposing urges, staying small versus growing bigger, are at loggerheads. It's an internal tug-of-war and can be exhausting. Sometimes one side wins, sometimes the other. The emotional back-and-forth leaves me unfocused and unable to make real goals for myself. It clouds my intentions and saps my energy.

Whew.

My solution at the moment: move beyond the focus on numbers and understand my true motivations. To redefine both ideas for myself. What do these things mean for me? How can I align with both of them?

Asking these questions means I have to dig beneath the easy answers. That's when things start to get interesting.

What do I value about small?

For me, staying small means staying real. Keeping myself honest, reminding myself to remain vulnerable.

That means remembering how much I don't know. Avoiding posing as the expert in the room, even as I learn all over again how to acknowledge and embrace my own authentic experiences. I can't tell you what we're supposed to be doing here, but I do know I've been through some stuff. I bet you have as well.

Through my words, I want to make a space for us to not know together. And to slowly, post by post, person by person, encourage all of us to get more comfortable with not knowing more than we know. It's a humble goal, creating and holding that space, but it feels like something I truly want to do and can keep doing for a long time. Sustainability is important.

Yet, what do I value about growing bigger?

While I feel the draw of numbers, I know there's more to it than stats. Perhaps growing can be reframed to mean experimenting. Writing longer posts. Stretching in new directions thematically. Adding in new links, audio, or other fun things. Trying stuff. Testing headlines. Exploring how prose might be shaped like a poem, and what variations on that question are possible? When do we throw grammatical rules to the side?

Growing can mean reaching for connections that move me beyond my own stack. Like writing this for SmallStack, for instance. Maybe growing bigger means growing in capacity from what I know, what I can do, what I've learned.

Understanding these deeper motivations, the tension between staying small and growing larger, resolves into intention (with the lovely play on words): to continue stretching myself in new directions, as they arise and feel right, and through this exploration and curiosity to stay vulnerable, connected, and in a place of "not knowing" and brave experiment.

In this, big and small work together to become complementary ideas that keep me right on the edge, exploring the liminal estuary spaces, where the most interesting things almost always happen.

Over at *An Inviting Space*, I believe reading is an interactive sport, and paid members receive a direct invitation to help them deepen into the material with every "small made thing" post. So, I leave you with an invitation to think about what these words and ideas mean for you, once we get past the headlines and the emotions and all the noise:

What is staying small and what is growing bigger for you, in your life today, where you are, as you are? What do these ideas mean for you? Where do they point? Maybe we're talking about writing. Maybe we're talking about creating. Maybe we're simply talking about getting from Wednesday to Thursday at our jobs, with our families, in our moments of solitude. How can those two opposing ideas be brought into connection and relationship? And once you've found that connection, what comes next?

What comes next? No matter how small or how big, that is always the question.

I can't wait to find out.

What monkeys can tell us about community

by Dr. Sanjida O'Connell

In the late afternoon, the baboons finally stopped and settled in the shade of an acacia tree. Sunlight glowed through the pods, turned the babies' protruding ears a delicate shell-pink and highlighted the wheat-blonde tips of their fur. I stopped a few metres away, thankful for the rest after following the troop since they'd risen at dawn. The babies played in the sand or suckled from their mothers; the rest of the troop paired up and took it in turns to groom each other. For the next hour they focused intensely as they combed through their partner's thick hair, touching lips gently to bare skin and emitting soft grunts.

For a few months before I started my PhD on chimpanzees, I helped on a research project in Namibia studying chacma baboons. Little did I know then that the data we were collecting would become part of a revolutionary new theory about the evolution of language and, ultimately, how many friends one can really have.

Even more astonishing was that those baboons, eking out their lives in the harsh Namib desert, would tell us how to run our Substacks three decades later.

How an arcane idea led to a revolutionary theory

My supervisor was Professor Robin Dunbar, who at the time was based at University College London before becoming an emeritus professor at Oxford University. In the dusty wood-panelled offices, we'd have lengthy discussions about grooming. Grooming in this context is literally a way of saying; I'll scratch your back, if you scratch mine. It removes parasites, but the main aim is touch, intimacy, stress-relief. It says: we're friends, I support you, I love you.

It's not just baboons that do it, it's all primates. However, it's not always equal. Some monkeys are groomed more than others. Some pairs groom each other more than they groom anyone else. Ultimately, grooming is the social glue that binds primates together.

What Robin was perplexed about was the amount of time primates spend grooming. Chacma baboons, for instance, can spend a fifth of their day grooming. It's costly behaviour: if you are grooming or being groomed, you can't eat... or do anything else. Primates (which includes us) are animals with big brains who live in complex social worlds. A big brain is also costly. A human brain, for instance, is nine times larger than any other mammal's if it were person-sized, and it takes 20% of our daily calories to simply keep it ticking over.

The discovery of a magic number

Suddenly, Robin had a light bulb moment as he realised that grooming is an extremely social behaviour. He put everything together—brain size, social group size in primates—and created a giant graph where he plotted the brain size of different primate species against grooming time, cross-checked with group size and—eureka! The larger the brain size, the larger the group size and the more time the animals had to spend grooming.[1]

As Robin told the Guardian: 'It was about 3am, and I thought, hmm, what happens if you plug humans into this?' According to the graph, for our brain size, we would live in groups of 150. 'It looked implausibly small, given that we all live in cities now,' Robin says, 'but it turned out that this was the size of a typical community in hunter-gatherer societies, and the average village size in the Domesday Book is also 150.'[2]

---

[1] Specifically it's the ratio of the volume of the neocortex to the rest of the brain, as the neocortex is the part of the brain involved in higher cognition and language, including skills such as working out who is friends with whom and then talking about them.

[2] "Robin Dunbar: We Can Only Ever Have 150 Friends at Most..." The Guardian, Guardian News and Media, 14 Mar. 2010, www.theguardian.com/technology/2010/mar/14/my-bright-idea-robin-dunbar.

The answer is 150.

In a nutshell, the more relationships you have, the bigger the group and the bigger the brain. But there's a trade-off—once you spend a quarter to a third of your day grooming, there just isn't enough time to eat, sleep, or do much else.

How grooming led to gossiping

Robin then hypothesised that language evolved as a way to 'groom' more than one person at once. Even better, it enabled our ancestors to multi-task—chat whilst foraging, hunting, or building a fire.

It might sound a little far-fetched, but Robin's analysis of what people spend most of their time talking about is other people. Language, Robin says, literally evolved so we can gossip.[3]

In his subsequent research he discovered that people, no matter their education or job, spent two-thirds of their conversations 'on matters of social import. Who is doing what with whom, and whether it's a good or a bad thing; who is in and who is out, and why.'

So, because we have large brains and we can chat to people in order to maintain our social relationships, we were able to live in relatively large groups—of 150 individuals. Although we're no longer hunter-gatherers, modern groups are similarly sized, whether it's the number of peo-

---

[3] Grooming, Gossip and the Evolution of Language by Robin Dunbar, 1996, Faber and Faber, London.

ple in an office, a factory, or a military faction. Even Christmas card lists fit this magic number.

'150 is the number of people you would not feel embarrassed about joining uninvited for a drink if you happened to bump into them in a bar.'[4]

How many friends can you really have?

Over the next few years, Robin finessed his magic number (which, in 2007, became known as Dunbar's Number). He discovered that 1500 is the limit of the number of people you can name.

You can also have 500 acquaintances, 50 people you'd call close friends—close enough to invite to dinner, say—15 in your close circle of friends; these are the people whom you turn to for sympathy and could confide in, 5 in your close support group, who are your best friends and most beloved family members.[5]

The layers are fluid—friendships change, people fall away or become closer—but the numbers remain the same.

What about social media?

Back then, when Robin was figuring this out and getting his PhD students to watch monkeys, social media was

[4] Konnikova, Maria. "The Limits of Friendship." The New Yorker, 7 Oct. 2014, www.newyorker.com/science/maria-konnikova/social-media-affect-math-dunbar-number-friendships.

[5] Friends: Understanding the Power of our Most Important Relationships by Robin Dunbar, 2021, Little Brown, London

barely a twinkle in Mark Zuckerberg's eye. The rise of Facebook, Twitter/X, Instagram and the rest of social media means that we can now monitor hundreds, if not thousands, of people. This is what Meta wants, isn't it? Likes and clicks and followers and friends. So surely, those numbers don't mean much now? Can you have more friends because of social media?

You lovely people are part of the SmallStack community. I think you know what I'm going to say. When all these naysayers (and Robin has done the number crunching, too) looked at the data gathered from social media users, they still found the same magic number: 150.

Research into Twitter/X shows that you can only follow 1 to 200 connections in a stable way over a period of a few months; a study of undergraduate Facebook users showed that no matter how many 'friends' the students had, they could only maintain close connections with 75. Even in online gaming—where games can encompass thousands globally—the same figures apply.

What do the numbers tell you?

This means that even on social media, you can only recognise up to 1500 of your followers. 500 will become acquaintances, and you'll be able to cultivate 100 to 200 real relationships with people, as you would if you lived in a village where everyone knows everyone else.

What social media can do is keep friendships alive that in pre-digital times might have died out, as Robin told

MIT Technology Review.[6] However, according to my old supervisor, it is no substitute for meeting face-to-face. 'It's extremely hard to cry on a virtual shoulder,' he dead-panned to the BBC. 'There is,' he says, 'no substitute for touch.'[7]

How does this affect Substack?

Even on Substack, the largest Substackers offer face-to-face meetings: Emma Gannon, who runs *The Hyphen* (with over 49,000 subscribers), recently held her first podcast for Substack in person. It was attended by 70 of her subscribers. She interviewed Farrah Storr of *Things Worth Knowing* (over 42,000 subscribers), whose own subscribers independently arranged to meet up before the event.

For me personally, I've been a little upset that one of the mega-Substackers didn't have any idea who I was in spite of me having attended two masterclasses, an online Zoom meet-up where I introduced myself, posting frequent comments, restacking of notes, and sending several emails (they said, *not sure who they are*, in the email so I know I'm not being hypersensitive!). I'm sure some of you

---

[6] Knight, Will. "Three Questions for Robin Dunbar." MIT Technology Review, MIT Technology Review, 2 Apr. 2020, www.technologyreview.com/2012/07/12/19077/three-questions-for-robin-dunbar/.

[7] "Dunbar's Number: Why We Can Only Maintain 150 Relationships." BBC News, BBC, 24 Feb. 2022, www.bbc.com/future/article/20191001-dunbars-number-why-we-can-only-maintain-150-relationships.

have had similar experiences. Reminding myself of Robin Dunbar's numbers makes me feel less hurt or judgmental. You just can't know or even recognise everyone if you're a BigStack.

For the SmallStack audience, I think this research is wonderful news. We are naturally going to be able to form deep and intimate connections with some of our subscribers. We are, by definition, going to know everyone who subscribes to us as an individual. Of course, some of us want to grow and will grow, but I would urge everyone here to remember these numbers. There are only so many people, even in the virtual world, we can truly be friends with.

Above all, let us remember: small is beautiful.

Small is where the best connections are made

by Sarah Teresa Cook

Last week, I started making sense of an idea I'd been carrying around for months. Picture it: A writer's club, but specifically for us neurodivergent folks who wish to tend and grow a strengths-based writing practice that accounts for our full selves; our craft and our joy, our goals and our needs.

Channeling all my descriptive powers, I opened my laptop and started thinking about the things that drive my teaching and space-holding philosophies. Certain go-to words showed up right away. Tender. Intersectional. Belongingness. Reciprocity. Yes yes: all good terms. And alongside them, a surprising and insistent one: Small.

I found myself writing about a "small" club for a "small" community, where we could have "small" experiences together. It was my first draft, but the word felt adamant. I impulsively listed a cap of 10 participants. Then I wrote a strange thing about having a true sliding scale; participants, I envisioned, could pay anywhere from zero dollars up to the full amount.

I paused. I noticed how good I felt, how clear. I messaged Robin: I think this has something to do with you, that your project has influenced me. Something new had entered my vocabulary. New-but-old. It felt like maybe I'd never used the word "small" before. And it felt like maybe the trajectories of my personal life and my professional life, and all these goals I've been setting and scrambling toward, were lining up around one singular idea. That small can be worthy.

Small is real

New-but-old is a feeling I've been steeped in for months now. New-but-old is what was conjured inside my body when my therapist first uttered the word, "Autism," last winter, and I had, for the first time in 36 years, a grasp on my own internal reality.

New-but-old is what I feel every time I'm picking up a cool insect and doing an okay job at guessing what it might be, or reading a sentence that bowls me over, or hiking somewhere in the Columbia River Gorge.

New-but-old is what I felt when I read about Robin's SmallStack project: This radical notion that something small isn't automatically bad or limited or a failure. If you spend even a fraction of your human time on social media, or you find yourself in the business of thinking about income and creativity in the same thoughts, you know what those disparaging words are pointing at.

A small number of followers. A small number of likes. A small program launch. A small *GASP* amount of money.

You don't have to be self-employed to be deeply, destructively influenced by big business rhetoric and capitalist expectations—and I suspect us neurodivergent folks are extra vulnerable here—that trick you into wishing constantly and only for bigger achievements. That you'll go viral. That you'll become rich. That you'll finally be known by floods of people, your name and image swallowed up whole in the mouths of those who know your content. But do they know you?

And it felt like maybe the trajectories of my personal life and my professional life, and all these goals I've been setting and scrambling toward, were lining up around one singular idea. That small can be worthy.

Small is knowable

I've always been confused by the language in certain calls for submissions, especially the ones geared toward writers who haven't yet published a full-length manuscript. Attention emerging writers! the calls read, again and again. Emerging from what? I know what they mean, but I don't understand it. What they mean is: Maggie

Smith and George Saunders and Margaret Atwood are known writers.

What they mean is Sarah Teresa Cook is not a known writer.

Yet with some frequency, I get emails or messages from others, telling me that something I've written has had a positive impact on them or made them feel seen. And almost 300 people have taken a moment out of their finite time on this planet to say, yes, I'd like to receive the fruits of your creative labor in my crowded, noisy inbox, a handful of them even willing to pay me money in exchange for it. And I've published enough chapbooks to not remember how many chapbooks I've published, a direct result of approximately 34 years of writing experience.

"You have to already be a known quantity," my partner laments every time he hears a too-common story about a good writer with a good manuscript who can't get their book published.

I'm not interested in arguing that big achievements are objectively bad ones. But I am very, very interested in what happens to our sense of self, let alone our belief in our creative and writerly impulses, when we give too much attention to a version of success that can only be satisfied by rapid, gigantic achievements.

Small is sacred

I realize I'm doing what I always do, trying to write about one thing—in this case, smallness—only to find that I can't do it without writing about many. Is this ironic? My attention sprawls, growths lengthy. Gets big in order to get its footing around something small.

But I think it's all connected, as I think most things are—autism; publishing; the ongoing work of wrangling myself out of terms that don't hold me anymore, in order to put my body near the ones that do. More irony: I am better held by small notions of success than big ones.

Are you? Well, have you asked yourself?

Small makes space for authenticity, integrity, and reciprocity. Small lets multiple people see and respond to each other in real time. Small facilitates mutual witnessing.

Reciprocity, mutuality... These are the words I am tired of sacrificing. I am tired of sacrificing the sincere joys of a small, mundane life at the Altar of Acclaim. There's something so healing, I told Robin, about seeing someone casually describe small things as valuable.

Small is where all the best connections are made. The intimate conversations. The tender one-on-one interactions. We make ourselves small enough—we get on our hands and knees if we must!—in order to peer at the stems and the dirt, and we imagine all the microorganisms rumbling and intersecting underground, nourishing the blessed soil. There's another word for this kind of small: Sacred.

It's okay to be known by a small number of people, to have a small number of readers, a small number of friends.

You are known by the people who know you. And so: you are known! Fully emerged. What you're doing counts.

You count.

I value smallness because I value the reality it affirms. Real people building real relationships, carefully and over time. People who grow like plants. We seem very still most of the time, yet here we are. Blooming.

The stay small recipe

by Rachel Shenk

I had not seen the woman approach the outdoor table where I sat with my siblings until she stood there, hopeful.

"Are you Rachel?" she asked.

"Yes," I replied as I took in the white covering with strings on her head and the plain dress, which told me she was Amish.

"I love your column! It is so calming. It reminds me to slow down and take the time away from my tasks. Thank you!" she said.

Taken by surprise, I managed a "Thank you for reading" as I shook her hand. Throughout the next week, I returned to that moment. To have a personal contact with a reader is a big thing. It gives me a window into who might be reading my words and reminds me that what I write has meaning beyond myself. To know my audience, and to remember their stories as I tell my own, changes me as a writer. And that's one of the reasons I've focused on staying small here on Substack.

There's an unwritten rule in my Midwestern American town. It tells me if I start any business endeavor that seems even mildly successful, the only way forward is to get bigger. "Grow the Business." When put into practice, this usually involves hiring folks to do the work you first started doing, turning yourself into a manager or boss, involving yourself in an institutional network, taking on added debt and risk.

In my life work, I was one of those Midwestern startups. I love baking and, after being fired from my job as an archivist, I took my passion and turned it into a business. Rachel's Bread grew from my small kitchen to become a brick-and-mortar artisan bakery beside our local farmers' market. With a joyful staff of ten, I made pastries as well as bread and pizzas in the wood-fired oven. Over the years, people would say, "You need to franchise this"; "You need more locations"; "Can I become an investor?"; "You need to find some wholesale accounts!"

Meanwhile, I just plodded along baking bread for the local community. I loved having my hands in the dough, chatting and hearing my customers' stories, and, most importantly, knowing all the small things that made the bakery successful. I never wanted to get bigger because I knew that with increased size there would also be compromise:

in relationships, in quality, in human connection, in authenticity.

My intention was never to be bigger. I was mainly hoping to have work that made me happy and gave me enough income to live sustainably. I wanted to grow the community in our town rather than grow the bakery. I often spoke of the bakery as a church, a place that brings diverse people together around a common love.

I no longer have the bakery. I retired from it after 25 years. But the bakery community is still strong.

As a new writer on Substack, I sensed that same "Get Bigger" rule. When I first joined, I seemed to be swamped with Notes about growth and how to develop high visibility and subscriber numbers. The thing is, that's not why I started writing and that's not why I started a Substack. I actually began *La Bonne Vie* as a column for a regional newspaper hoping I could connect with a small group of local readers.

In joining Substack, I hoped to broaden my audience and make a little money with my writing. But my main goal here remains the same as at the bakery: To stay small by building community and human connection rather than focusing on numbers or dollars. To bring people together in a kind of church of writing.

Here's my bakery's Stay Small recipe that I now use on Substack, with a few notes below.

> 2 cups Quality
> 2 cups Generosity
> 1 cup Sustainability
> 3 cups Community
> 2 tablespoons zest of Vision
> 2 slivers of Authenticity
> 1 tablespoon juice of Selfishness
> 3 pinches of Magic

Mix these together as needed. Add a few grinds of Hard Parts. Bake into a cohesive whole and share profusely.

Quality

At the bakery, I refused to compromise on the ingredients. I never looked for the cheapest chocolate chips or flour. I made small batches by hand to ensure the best flavor.

In writing, I think through each column. I fashion each one with care. I take the time I need to write. I don't turn my writing into a product. I don't use AI.

Generosity

At the bakery, I often gave an extra free cookie or croissant to a customer. I hosted a free annual feast for customers. In a world where almost nothing is given away without something in return, I offered what I could freely.

In my writing, I have chosen not to paywall my posts. Those who choose to pay for my writing are doing so by choice. I've sent each of my paying subscribers a small handmade block print or self-published book as a thank you. I write with a generous spirit.

Sustainability

At the bakery, I tried to make my work sustainable rather than profit-oriented. I took time off regularly as a way to control the stress of hard work and as a means to renew my creativity. I didn't let the business control me.

In my writing, I take time off if I need to. I don't let the deadlines or the readers control me or my writing. I resist the pressures of an online presence.

Community

At the bakery, I tried to create a safe place where everyone felt included, where people were heard, where people could meet. I knew most of my customers by name or sight. I never had to advertise; the business grew slowly by word of mouth.

In my writing, I encourage community. I write as just one human to another, not as an expert. I write about the small things around us that matter. I keep my readers' stories, many whom I know, in the forefront as I write. I respond to comments on my posts. I am growing slowly as readers find me.

Vision

At the bakery, I tried to always keep a balanced view of both the forest and the trees. To keep the baking at the forefront and yet tie it into the larger community, sustenance for the body and the soul.

In my writing, I focus on the small things that can make a difference in the larger world. I try to connect our daily gestures to a broader understanding of life.

Authenticity

At the bakery, I didn't take on a role. I was always myself. In situations where people would try to make me be someone else, I refused. I stayed true to my core.

In my writing, I don't play games. I choose honesty and hope over insincerity and cynicism.

Selfishness

Okay. Maybe you weren't expecting this one. I love baking bread and having a bakery was what I wanted to do. I often told customers that I felt selfish doing what I loved rather than thinking of it as working for someone else. But that self-love is how love is then passed on to others. Loving what I did allowed me to care about others.

In my writing, I acknowledge that I am fortunate to have readers who read my columns and even comment about them! I tell them that they are essential to my work. I look for connections that make me a better writer. I focus on topics that I am familiar with and have lived. And hope my readers can find a bit of themselves in my column as well.

Magic

In both my baking and my writing, I've encountered what I call magic. That intangible moment that creates a connection with the customer or reader. I only have these tips to encourage the magic:

Pay attention. Continuously.
Look for it. Continuously.
Work with love. Continuously.

The Hard Part

At the bakery, I felt the pressures of expectations from those who did not understand why I remained small. I had to hold my ground against assumptions and gossip. I had to learn to let go of worries about making ends meet. I had to educate folks about the benefits of being small.

In my writing, I can be blinded by the "Big Stacks" who advertise their large, seemingly easy-to-get subscribers. I try to avoid those offering "best tips" and focus on my own writing. I have to accept that I'm a small fish in a huge sea. I have to remain true to my vision despite alluring calls from Notes. I need to remind myself that what I write has value even if no one responds.

It's been seven years since I left the bakery and yet I still receive thank you's, I still hear stories, I still feel the love from former customers. And it's because they learned through my work that one baker with small dreams can have an enormous impact in ways they might never have thought of.

I intend to continue writing *La Bonne Vie* in the same way. Just one columnist with small dreams focused on the small things that, I hope, will connect with at least one reader out there. And I hope this post will encourage you to do the same.

It's the small things that make me happy.

Afterword

I have tried multiple times, in multiple ways, to craft the right opening to this essay. With each attempt, a voice whispers in my head: *Who am I to do this work? What do I know about publishing, much less publishing an anthology? I lack the schooling, the credentials, and the relevant experience. I don't belong here.*

Yet here I am, to my own great astonishment, and here you are, sharing this moment with me across time and ink and paper, reading these hard-won words and giving me hope that somehow, it worked out. Somehow, I and we and this book muddled through together and found a place on your shelf. For that, and you, I am endlessly grateful.

I grew up in a house on a hill in the heart of an enchanted forest. I was a shy, chubby kid who loved fairy tales and hated sports. I'm sure I don't have to name the ways that shy, chubby kids who love fairy tales and hate sports are told they don't belong. I heard them, loud and quiet. Thank goodness I heard the trees and wildflowers, too.

I measured time by the school year, yes, but also by the seasons that bloomed and buzzed upon my hill. Fall was a time not only for books and new clothes but also bronzed oak leaves and bright madrone berries, life bursting its last before the long, gray sleep of winter. I knew the first spring beauties would bloom in late February, followed by butter-cups and shooting stars, jewel-like in the underbrush. Summer brought spotted fawns, elegant irises and, on very lucky days, bits of speckled robin's egg from a long-abandoned nest.

My hill was the first, and, for a long time, the only place where I knew unconditional belonging. My own insecuri-ties aside, I have found it again in this book and the dream we are building.

My part in Small Robin Press began with a thought, a small and terribly reckless thought that morphed into a grand and terribly reckless dream to, well, to do lots of things, actually, but mostly, to tell stories—specifically, the sorts of stories that are unlikely to be told elsewhere. Tra-ditional publishing rarely wants small voices, especially those on the margins. It's far more profitable to invest in big, popular names with big, popular platforms that satisfy shareholders and guarantee book sales.

And those who can't or won't walk that path, who pour their words into the void on faith and talent alone? Could a home exist for those voices, too? Not only a home, but a safe and nurturing space—dare I say, a nest—that helps small authors spread their wings?

Reckless thoughts, indeed.

It all started one sunny day in May. I was out for a walk, enjoying the warm weather and the sun on my face, looking, as always, for any neighborhood cat friends who wanted to say hello, when my synapses conspired to form the words, *I should volunteer to help with SmallStack.*

The concept of SmallStack—a library created by and for Substack authors with fewer than 1,000 subscribers—was barely out of infancy, born of a single post from Robin Taylor that went viral on a wave of pent-up frustration (Substack, like most platforms, favors the famous). I and nearly 2,000 others loved the idea and signed up, and suddenly Robin had a second full-time job on his hands. He was overwhelmed, and I realized I could help.

The desire to join SmallStack rang through my spirit like a bell. I felt the weight of it in my bones. But could I trust it? Was I really willing to commit the time and effort to build an online library, of all things? Like many dreamers, I have wild thoughts all the time. They often hit hard at first, only to fade upon further reflection. This thought, though, this persuasive, pesky, beautiful, reckless thought refused to go away. It wore at my defenses like water wears through stone, revealing a depth of yearning I didn't know I felt—to write, to be seen, to belong.

On May 29, 2024, I sent Robin a message and offered to help shepherd the SmallStack library into being. At this point, I knew him primarily as a cool guy who wrote thoughtful essays and with whom I happened to share a first name (that's kind of a big deal, actually—there aren't that many Robins in the world). We had a few mutual connections and had exchanged a passing comment or two, but we were essentially strangers. I laid out my case carefully—marketing background, highly organized, deep belief in the mission—and awaited his reply with butterflies in my stomach. *Please let me belong here*, said the lonely child in me. *Please believe I'm enough.*

A few days later, we had a video call, and we learned that in addition to sharing a first name, we shared a time zone, a love of gardening, and a deep, immediate connection (I didn't mention the latter at the time, afraid of sounding weird, but upon ending the call, I remember thinking very clearly that I had just made a soul friend). Thus we became "the Robins" of SmallStack and set out to build a library. We assembled a team of volunteers and learned a great deal about Notion. We launched the series of guest posts that would one day become this very anthology you now hold in your hands. We painstakingly updated spreadsheets, said farewell to beloved pets, survived career transitions, and vented about editorial snafus. We shared our fears for the future. We gave voice to our secret dreams.

Even then, we knew we were building more than a library. The shape of something bigger hovered just out of sight, a felt sense of possibility we couldn't yet name. We talked about it sometimes. I knew Robin dreamed of starting a publishing company one day—a gorgeous and tender dream of lifting up small voices, of creating a space where writers without large platforms and Big Five book deals, who had perhaps looked at traditional publishing and thought, *I don't belong here,* could find a home that would let their words take wing. A dream that felt very far away until we realized we'd been planting the seeds for Small Robin Press all along.

I know well the power of seeds.

When I was eight years old, I discovered a new flower upon my hill, vibrant pink with five delicate petals. I was near our cluster of fruit trees, a place I wandered frequently, so I knew this flower hadn't been there last year. It felt like a gift, a fae offering for a lonely child who loved her forest. There was only the one, so I left it alone (it's a sacred rule to never, ever pick the last flower). Later, I flipped through my parents' wildflower book and learned its name was checkermallow, a name right out of fairyland. I returned next year, and to my delight, two checkermallows smiled up at me. Two became several, and several become dozens. By the time I left for college, stalks of bold pink checkermallows bloomed all over the lower half of my hill—all from one small flower, and perhaps a little help from the robins.

On June 20, 2025, the words "Small Robin Press" were uttered aloud for the first time. They fluttered in my throat, my heart, and I knew. I looked at Robin. He looked at me. And here we are.

Robin Cangie, Small Robin Press Co-founder

Contributors

KATE BRENNAN is an artist, educator and creator. She has written a dozen plays and musicals and has taught across the country. She has been named a three-time O'Neill Semifinalist, a Princess Grace Finalist, a Judith Royer Finalist, a Jane Chambers Finalist, a Cultural Alliance Artist Innovator Award Finalist, and a Jonathan Larson Grant Finalist. Kate is a Designated Linklater Teacher and holds an MFA from UVA. She writes the Substack *More Humor More Humanity*. Check out her creativity book, *How to Dramadoodle*.
@KateEmoryCreates, KateBrennan.org

SARAH TERESA COOK is a writer and creative mentor whose work explores memory, language, and the porous boundaries between imagination and authenticity. She publishes *For the Birds*, a newsletter about creativity and neurodivergence. Her writing has appeared in *Hobart*

Pulp, *Write or Die Magazine*, *Porterhouse Review*, *Oregon Humanities Magazine*, and *Spoon Knife*. She loves film cameras, bugs, and rewatching Gilmore Girls for comfort research. Learn more at SarahTeresaCook.com.

AMANDA GIBSON is a former nurse turned blog writer who shares raw reflections on life with the autoimmune condition ankylosing spondylitis, a rare and often misdiagnosed form of inflammatory arthritis. Through her Substack blog *In My Bones*, Amanda writes to connect, comfort, and create community for others living with chronic illness. She's passionate about raising awareness of this little-known condition to help shorten the diagnostic journey for others. When she's not writing, she's off adventuring in a campervan with her husband and their cheeky black Labrador, Winnie, chasing moments that remind her what she's fighting for.

DR. SANJIDA O'CONNELL has a PhD in zoology and psychology. She's the author of eight novels and four non-fiction books. Sanjida previously worked as a wildlife presenter for the BBC and an environmental features writer and columnist for national newspapers and magazines. She writes psychological thrillers under the pen name of Sanjida Kay: *Bone by Bone*, *The Stolen Child*, *My Mother's Secret*, and *One Year Later*, were all published by Corvus Books. Her short stories have been featured on BBC Radio

4, in *The Perfect Crime* (Harper Collins), *The Book of Bristol,* and *The Monster, Anthology* (Comma Press).

Sanjida has been shortlisted for the BBC Asia Awards, the Betty Trask Award for Romantic Fiction, the Daily Telegraph Science Writer's Award, Asian Woman of the Year, highly commended for BBC Wildlife Magazine's Award for Nature Writing, long-listed for the CWA Steel Dagger, shortlisted for CWA Short Story Dagger, and won the CWA Short Story Dagger.

She writes a Substack newsletter called *Wild Writing with Sanjida*, teaching writers who want to be published, and has just finished a nature memoir called *Wilderness: In Search of Belonging.*

SARAH SADIE is a poet, writer, and creative visionary who lives on a continental divide in a small town in Wisconsin. Winner of the Lorine Niedecker Prize, the Posner Prize and a Pushcart Prize, she grows tomatoes in buckets and teaches and facilitates workshops and classes with the aim of helping creatives find their new stories and next steps. Her poetry has been published widely and collected into five books including a letter press edition from Red Dragonfly Press. Online, she can be found holding *An Inviting Space* on Substack where she shares reflections, invitations and prompts with her readers and hosts an ever growing circle of creative practitioners, artists, and writers. AnInvitingSpace.substack.com

RACHEL SHENK, born and raised in Belgium with detours to Spain and Scotland, was an artisan baker for 30 years in a small Midwestern U.S. town. Her weekly column, *La Bonne Vie*, in print in The Goshen News since 2006, and on Substack since 2024, shares stories and thoughts about the good life from her experiences. She's currently a cheesemonger at her local farmers' market, where she continues to sell bread and pastries. She's a traveler, a reader, a block printer, and is always up for cooking a delicious meal and sharing it with friends. She has self-published two books, *Cultured: Stories and Recipes from La Bonne Vie*, 2019, and *Rachel's Bread: The Cookbook*, 2017.

ALEXA SPIEGEL (she/her) is a recovering overachiever, an avid reader, a Leo Sun/Aquarius Moon/Scorpio Rising, and just recently gathered the courage to start calling herself a writer. After suffering from burnout and quitting a 12-year corporate career, she turned to writing as a way to "heal out loud" by sharing her most vulnerable thoughts with an internet full of strangers. You can find her on Substack where she writes *Sundays in high school*, a (semi)weekly newsletter dedicated to mental health, major life transitions, and navigating your 30s. Alexa resides in Long Beach, CA, with her husband, two spoiled cats, and a baby on the way.

JAMIE WALLACE is a Gen X writer on a creative journey back to herself. Coming off two decades as a freelance writer in the marketing space, she is now exploring more personal questions about creativity, happiness, and authenticity in her newsletter, *Inner Wilderness Unlimited*. Jamie writes about art, nature, community, curiosity, connection, and her experience as a human being with creative urges that aren't always easy to fit into Real Life.

When she's not writing, Jamie can be found experimenting with new art projects, riding horses, walking dogs, or talking to her cat, Cinder. She lives in a small, historic town north of Boston with her daughter and an embarrassingly large collections of books, rocks, and journals. Connect with her via her newsletter on Substack or on Instagram @SuddenlyJamie.

Acknowledgments

A thousand thank yous to the Small Robin Press Team—Erin Michaela Sweeney, Cheshir, Sue-Jan Noreiga, LC Sharkey, Nospheratt, Amanda Rose Fadely, Erin Mercer, Elizabeth Austin, and Elle Kennedy Fell—for all of the support, laughter, and joy you help bring into the world. It's difficult to imagine choosing to spend your free time editing essays, sending emails, and constructing digital work spaces, yet each of you appeared with innovative ideas and a helping hand when it was needed most.

This book was made possible by the ideas, creativity, and collective vision of the entire SmallStack and Small Robin Press community. It is with abundant joy that we print these words to preserve them for all the "smalls" yet to come.

Small Robin Press

Small Robin Press cares deeply about the power of small voices. We publish new and emerging writers, underrepresented authors, and folx from intersectional communities making big differences through small actions.

SmallRobinPress.com

small robin press

www.ingramcontent.com/pod-product-compliance
Lightning Source LLC
Chambersburg PA
CBHW051642120626
46551CB00015B/2188